Online College

What You Need to Know Before Beginning a Virtual Distance Learning Degree Program

by

Mark W. Timmis

author HOUSE

1663 LIBERTY DRIVE, SUITE 200
BLOOMINGTON, INDIANA 47403
(800) 839-8640
www.authorhouse.com

First published by AuthorHouse 06/07/04

ISBN: 1-4184-1154-X (e)
ISBN: 1-4184-1153-1 (sc)

Printed in the United States of America
Bloomington, Indiana

This book is printed on acid-free paper.

http://www.virtualcollege.info

Acknowledgements

A sincere debt of gratitude goes out to my wife Denise who kept everything running, which made it possible for me to continue my education, successfully complete the program, and get this book written.

Many thanks to Laura Bowman for editing this book and being so wonderful to work with.

A special thank-you to Lizette Downey for helping me to market the book, and Peggy Emard for being so supportive of my effort to write this book.

Table of Contents

Introduction

In the fall of 2001 I decided to return to college and get a degree in Information Technology (IT). My problem with returning to college was the 90-minute round trip drive to the downtown branch of our state college. While it is a fine institution, I just did not have time for that kind of drive, so I began to investigate online alternatives.

After investigating several different online schools I decided that the University of Phoenix offered the best program to suit my needs, but I was still a little skeptical about getting a degree online. I continued my exploration with questions to past alumni and some students still in the program, and they all had overwhelmingly positive things to say about this program and online college in general. After my employer agreed to pay the costs of schooling, and my wife agreed it was a good idea I signed up and began classes in November of 2001.

I decided to write this book because of the difficulty I had finding answers to the questions I had about getting a degree online. I wanted the nitty-gritty details if I was going to invest that much time, energy, and money in a degree program. I hope this book helps you to understand how the system works, and helps you feel comfortable about making your decision. All of the information in this book is from first-hand experience, and every attempt has been made to represent all activities as truthfully as possible. No glamorization's or misrepresentations were employed.

You may be interested in knowing that I did graduate with a Masters of Science in Computer Information Systems in October of 2003, just two years after beginning my program. While I am thankful for being gainfully employed in the IT arena, it would also be nice if this economy would turn around so that we all could enjoy a few more employment options. For more information on online college please visit http://www.virtualcollege.info.

Chapter 1:

Introduction to the Virtual College Experience

What makes online college classes different from traditional college or university classes?

Online classes draw upon each student's work experiences in the real world, much more than regular college classes. Since most students in the traditional college setting have not had to work, this only makes sense. Schools offering online classes have really used student work experience to their advantage. I learned a great deal from other students' work experiences that I might not otherwise have learned if the program had not been constructed in the manner that it was.

Online college classes are different from regular college classes in that the responsibility is completely on the student to do a lot more work in a self-directed environment. There is also less time to do the work, because each class is not the traditional 16 weeks in length. For instance, there is a great deal of reading in an online class, and since the class meets for 6 weeks instead of 16 weeks, it may appear that there is no way to complete all of the assigned reading. By not completing the scheduled reading, you hurt yourself more in the online class because of the brevity of the class and the reduced exposure to the subject.

Online classes allow students an unprecedented amount of flexibility regarding attendance, which can be set by each individual student. Classes over the Internet also eliminate drive times required by traditional college classes, and turn that time into valuable learning time. The rest of this book discusses the differences in detail.

Class meetings and length of classes

In a regular college class, you may attend class 32 to 48 times in one semester, depending upon whether you meet two or three days per week over a 16 week period of time. In an online program, classes may be as short as six weeks. Most online programs insist that you log in and participate five out of seven days per week, which would put you at 30 class meetings, and if you attend 7 days a week (which is your option) you are up to 42 class meetings. Since the actual amount of time spent in a traditional class occurs over a physically longer period of time, however, you may have more opportunities to pick up information by virtue of your proximity to that information over that extended period of time. In an online class, you may have to work harder because you need to understand the same amount of information in a shorter period of time.

Distance relationships versus personal relationships

One of the most interesting aspects of the online classroom is the relationships you develop with classmates. There is a true dichotomy to the notion of relationships in the online environment. One instructor that I had questioned whether these were really relationships at all since you would never know this person on the street. His question makes sense in many ways, but I actually had much more interaction with peers in an online environment than I ever had in a traditional classroom setting. I also learned a great deal vicariously from their shared life experiences. However, I did not form as many close relationships with people in my online classes as I did when I went to college in a brick-and-mortar institution.

In an online setting you get the 30,000-foot view of your classmates' lives from their three-paragraph autobiographies. This may not sound like much, but pick any class that you took in a brick-and-mortar institution and tell me how many people you even knew that much about? If you add the amount of time you spend with people on your team, and add to that the number of classes you may share with them, it is easy to get to know people fairly well. However, you never see what they look like, unless they include a picture, which some students do. I met a classmate for lunch one day. It was an enjoyable meeting, but my online perception of that person was very different from my in-person perception. Not better, not worse, just very different.

Chapter 2:

Why Online College is a Good Choice

Flexibility

Online college is a good choice for people with a lot of time constraints in their life. I personally selected an online program because it allowed me to be close to home to help care for my newborn child, and be able to have a lot of quality family time. I was able to achieve the family time, get an advanced degree, and work a full-time job. I never would have been able to do this if I had to drive to my local university, which is an hour round trip from my home. I was so grateful for the educational alternative, even though the program that I selected had a higher monetary cost; it gave me the ultimate amount of personal flexibility and enabled me to accomplish multiple tasks at the same time.

Ease of use

Online college is very easy to use. You do *not* need to be extremely adept with your computer to take classes online. All you need is a computer (desktop or laptop) with at least a 56Kbps modem and a dial-up connection and you are in business. As far as software, you need a copy of a word processing program (i.e., Microsoft Word), and software that allows you to access the classes, such as Microsoft Outlook Express, or whatever program the institution you select uses. There is the occasional class that uses other software, but you have plenty of warning about those classes, and can easily pick up a copy of the program(s) that you need.

Convenience

There is nothing easier than having everything you need at your fingertips. An online college program gives you this type of convenience. This makes going to school very easy, but you pay for it; online classes are expensive. Most schools know that people who want to go to school will pay for the convenience of being able to attend classes online, in the privacy of their own homes.

The flip side to the convenience of online college is that you need to be *self-motivated*. This point is easily the most important ingredient to being successful in an online degree program. If you are easily distracted by occurrences in your home setting, have too many other things going on in your life, or are not disciplined enough to focus on your schoolwork, then excelling in an online program may be impossible. I cannot stress this enough, this tip is very important. Which brings me to the next point: How much time is involved in an online class?

Chapter 3:

What Online College Programs Expect from You

How many hours a week are required for each class?

This was my primary question before I began online classes, but the real answer is that it depends a lot on the variables — the instructor, the class, and you. You may spend anywhere from 10 to 30 hours a week at the low and high ranges. If I did spend 30 hours working on schoolwork in one week, I can assure you that it was not consistent. The average was more like 20 hours per week. If a class is six weeks long, the first week may require 15 hours, of which 5 or more may be for reading the text. The second through fifth weeks may require 20 or more hours, depending upon how much time you spend reading and writing. If you can read most of your texts before the class starts, then your time per week will probably average 15 to 20 hours, but if you are reading the text as

9

you go along, that could boost the time spent on schoolwork each week by approximately 5 hours.

There is really a lot of work in an online program. There is a great deal of reading, and an enormous amount of writing.

How much reading is assigned?

Two different textbooks are usually used for each class. At first I thought this was ridiculous, but I now realize the value of this. Each text has a different vantage point and strength, and 90 percent of the time there is little or no redundancy. In fact, there are texts that are well worth rereading just to glean a bit more information from them.

In addition to the two textbooks, you need to read the messages in the newsgroups from your classmates, which easily add up to 30 to 60 minutes of reading per day. There are also approximately five or six magazine articles to read, which are provided by the university. Usually at least two magazine articles are assigned per week, which adds about 15 minutes of reading per week. You may also have to read a lecture by the instructor every week (5–10 typewritten pages), and the syllabus (10 typewritten pages). Additionally, you may have books to read on pertinent topics, depending upon what types of writing projects that you have due. If you do not read fast now, you probably will after the first few classes.

Do you take tests?

There are occasional tests, but as a whole they are few and far between. Tests may be open book, but as you probably know, most open book tests tend to be difficult and make you work a bit harder.

How much writing is involved?

There is a great deal of writing in online college classes; not all of it has to do with writing papers, but much of it does. In the classes I was enrolled in, there was a paper due every week, except the first week of class. The APA format was generally the format of choice by most instructors, but occasionally the MLA format was required. The weekly papers were never very long, approximately 275 to 325 words per page; four pages long was the general length (six total with the title and bibliography pages).

In addition to the weekly papers and finals, you have to respond to at least two newsgroup postings per day with a substantial contribution, which is considered to be around 100 written words of meaningful discussion on a specific topic. In my classes, there were approximately five Discussion Questions offered each week, and I was required to respond to three. Each Discussion Question response was in the range of 100 to 300 words, occasionally more. Another required document for each class was a Weekly Summary highlighting the things that you learned throughout the week; this document was recommended to be 300 to 500 words.

Team papers are due weekly, and if everyone works together contributing one or two pages each, this is usually enough to satisfy the weekly team assignment.

The final paper is part of the final team assignment, which may be a long paper (12–15 pages or more). A compilation of team assignments, with the addition of a small amount of new information (and a lot of polish), is usually sufficient. A PowerPoint presentation that summarizes the team paper is also a requirement for the final team assignment.

Chapter 4:

The Format of an Online Class

How are online classes structured and delivered?

At a popular online university, the classes are delivered through Outlook Express (OE), which I was skeptical about at the very beginning. However, OE proved to be an excellent tool for this application. The university Information Technology department sets up a Web page for each student that contains personal and school-related information. It also contains an auto-setup link to set up your Outlook Express folders for the current class that you are taking.

All classes can be accessed from either the Web or OE. I prefer OE because it allows you to see the message threads as they are sent, and respond to them accordingly. Access through the Web page only allows you to see the messages chronologically. This is a disadvantage, because you may not see how a message is contextually referenced by other messages in the message thread. Since most instructors want you to respond to a particular number of threads per day, it is better to have as much information as possible to help you form a clear picture of the direction of the thread. Some days it is difficult to meet the minimum number of online interactions, so any advantage helps.

Newsgroups

All of my classes had eight newsgroup folders, and each folder contained newsgroup messages that pertained to some aspect of the class. Figure 1 illustrates the class folder structure. The class folders listed under the primary folder, MSCIS, are as follows:

- The top folder under the MSCIS folder is the primary classroom newsgroup folder where all class interactions take place. You can submit messages to this folder, and see all of the messages sent by your classmates.

- The Assignments newsgroup folder is a write-only folder, meaning that you can submit messages with attachments to this folder (usually your papers and other assignments for grading purposes), but you cannot see the contents of this folder. Only the instructors have read and write access to this folder.

- The Chat Room newsgroup folder is like a student lounge area for students to discuss ideas that are interesting, but the topics may not pertain to the class.

- The Course Materials newsgroup folder is used by the instructor to post items, and by the students to download information. This typically includes instruction items and messages from the instructor, such as class rules, the class syllabus, weekly assignments, errors, last-minute changes, and other information pertinent to completing the class successfully.

- Then there are four Learning Team newsgroup folders. During the first or second week of class, the instructor forms the learning teams and each team is assigned a folder (A, B, C, or D). In most classes, folder D is never used. Usually instructors do not want learning teams viewing each other's work, so occasionally the instructor requests that you delete the other folders for teams of which you are not a member.

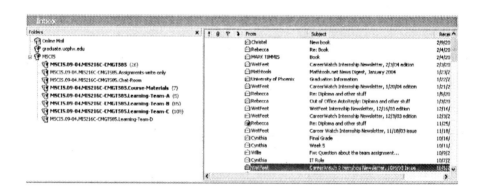

Figure 1: Newsgroup folders in the Outlook Express interface.

It is important to stay on the topic of discussion in the primary classroom newsgroup, and to try to make your message as pertinent as possible. This is difficult at times, because you may only be able to relate a similar, but not exact, experience, or you may have no direct experience to relate, but it is still important to

18

try. It is also important to maintain the integrity of the newsgroups as they are applied. Professionalism and common courtesies should be the norm for all of your newsgroup interactions. This ideal is easy to maintain most of the time, however, occasional team problems may challenge this ideal communication format.

Chapter 5:

Detailed Overview of a Typical Class

What is a typical online class like?

I attended a popular online university and can only speak about their classes, which are six full weeks in length. The school week is from Thursday (Day 1) through Wednesday (Day 7) of the following week. If possible, before the class meets, try to download the materials that are available, such as the books, syllabus, and magazine articles that you will need to read — and start reading! Sometimes you also can anticipate the need for other materials. I recommend a trip to your public library to pick up materials that are pertinent to the class, because they may be useful when writing a paper or answering Discussion Questions.

The following outline is a sample class schedule:

Week 1

Day 1 (Thursday)

- Meet and greet the instructor and your classmates. Go to the classroom newsgroup and read all of the information posted by the instructor. Then post a short biography about yourself in the location determined by the instructor. It is good professional practice to respond to each of your classmates' biographies as well. This helps develop rapport, and gets the class off to a good start.

- Download the syllabus and any other materials published by the instructor.

- Check for a class schedule (see Figure 2). If the instructor does not provide one, then you may want to create one. It will help you to keep due dates and assignments straight.

- Read the materials for class, then, if you haven't started already, start reading the text!

Day 2 (Friday)

- Check the classroom newsgroup; you may need to respond to your classmates' responses to your autobiography.

- Is there anything due? It is unlikely on the second day, but you may have something due on the third day — a Discussion Question or two? Check those and begin thinking about your responses.

- Read!

Day 3 (Saturday)

- Check the classroom newsgroup; you may need to respond to your classmates' responses to your autobiography.

- Write and post responses to the Discussion Questions.

- Read!

Day 4 (Sunday)

- Check the classroom newsgroup; you may need to respond to your classmates' responses to the Discussion Questions.

- Post responses to the remaining Discussion Questions.

- Choose a team. See what teams are available and what topic they focus on, and choose by topic. You may be assigned to a team according to your time zone.

- Read!

Day 5 (Monday)

- Check the classroom newsgroup; you may need to respond to your classmates' responses to the Discussion Questions.

- Check to see when your first paper is due. Most likely there will be a paper due on the same day every week! This gives everyone a chance to plan ahead.

- Meet and greet your team members.

- Read!

Day 6 (Tuesday)

- Check the classroom newsgroup; you may need to respond to your classmates' responses to the Discussion Questions.

- Tuesday is frequently the day that papers are due, but not always. Submit your paper, but be sure that you post it to the correct newsgroup folder.

- Is anything due tomorrow? How about that Learning Summary? Write the Learning Summary.

- Read!

Day 7 (Wednesday)

- Check the classroom newsgroup; you may need to respond to your classmates' responses to the Discussion Questions.

- Submit the Learning Summary to the correct newsgroup folder.

- Read!

Week 2

Day 8 (Thursday) — *Beginning of Week 2!*

- Check the classroom newsgroup; you may need to respond to your classmates' responses to the Learning Summary.

- Check the team newsgroup, and participate as necessary.

- Download and read this week's lecture.

- Check the syllabus, or class schedule, to ensure that you know what is due this week, and can plan out your week.

- Read over the Discussion Questions. Can you respond to the Discussion Questions without doing research? If so, write your responses, but do not submit them until they are due. If not, start looking up sources to prepare to write responses.

- Read!

Day 9 (Friday)

- Take the day off from the classroom newsgroup.

- Check the team newsgroup, and participate as necessary.

- Write your responses to all of the Discussion Questions, if you have not done so.

- Do you have a paper due this week? If so, can you write it without doing research? If not, get on the Internet and start looking up sources, or go to your neighborhood public library and find materials.

- Read, if necessary.

Day 10 (Saturday)

- Post whatever Discussion Questions are due today, and respond to your classmates' responses to the Discussion Questions.

- Check the team newsgroup, and participate as necessary.

- Write your paper, if you have not done so.

  o Do not forget sources.

  o Is the paper finished? If so, submit it to the writing lab to have them check for grammar. It does not cost anything, and it may get you a few extra points.

- Read, if necessary.

Day 11 (Sunday)

- Take the day off from the primary classroom newsgroup, but post any assignments that are due.

- Check the team newsgroup, and participate as necessary.

- Finish your paper, if you have not done so.

- Read, if necessary.

Day 12 (Monday)

- Check the classroom newsgroup; turn in assignments that are due, and respond to your classmates' responses to the Discussion Questions.

- Check the team newsgroup, and participate as necessary.

- Revise your paper when it comes back from the writing lab.

- Read, if necessary.

Day 13 (Tuesday)

- Check the classroom newsgroup; turn in assignments that are due, and respond to your classmates' responses to the Discussion Questions.

- Check the team newsgroup, and participate as necessary.

- Submit your paper, but be sure that you post it to the correct newsgroup folder.

- Read magazine articles and write your Learning Summary.

- Read, if necessary.

Day 14 (Wednesday)

- Check the classroom newsgroup; turn in assignments that are due, and respond to your classmates' responses to the Discussion Questions.

- Check the team newsgroup, and participate as necessary.

- Post the Learning Summary to the correct newsgroup folder.

- Read, if necessary.

Week 2 is typical of all weeks except the first and last, so Week 2 can be referred to for Weeks 3, 4, and 5. I will attempt to describe Week 6 because it can get a little harried sometimes.

Usually most instructors follow a different protocol for Week 6, but some do not. Frequently, the Discussion Questions are suspended if team activities are particularly intense, but do not count on that. Also, you may not have an individual paper due because each team will have at least two assignments due: a comprehensive "Final" paper and a corresponding PowerPoint presentation that summarizes the paper; however, not having an individual final is discretionary. The most important aspect of the final week is to know when everything is due, and make sure that your teammates are also aware of this so that everyone can plan accordingly and participate equally in the preparation of the final. Communication is essential because some people like to wait until the last minute to do critical work, which may not allow an adequate amount of time to get the work completed to everyone's satisfaction, especially the instructors! Each team member is graded on their individual participation, willingness to work with other team members, their ability to work through problems, and getting the job done well. Frequently, your teammates are also given an opportunity to assess all team members for the final grade. Some instructors weigh this heavily!

Week 6

Day 36 (Thursday) — **Beginning of Week 6, and the end of the class!**

- Make a point of getting together with all of the team members to ensure that everyone is aware of the requirements and deadlines for the final assignments. Draft a schedule of required group activities and meeting times to complete the assignments, and assign responsibilities.

- Check the syllabus and schedule to ensure that you know what is due this week and plan out your week.

- If participation is mandatory for this week, check the classroom newsgroup, but if participation is not mandatory, suspend participation until it is required.

- Download this week's lecture, and read it.

- Read over the Discussion Questions. Can you respond to the Discussion Questions without doing research? If so, write your responses, but do not submit them until they are due. If not, start looking up sources to prepare for writing responses.

- Read!

Day 37 (Friday)

- Check the team newsgroup and work on team activities.

- Participate in the classroom newsgroup, if necessary.

- Submit all assignments that are due, but be sure that you post them to the correct newsgroup folder.

- Read, if necessary.

Day 38 (Saturday)

- Check the team newsgroup and work on team activities.

- Participate in the classroom newsgroup, if necessary.

- Submit all assignments that are due, but be sure that you post them to the correct newsgroup folder.

- Read, if necessary.

Day 39 (Sunday)

- Check the team newsgroup and work on team activities.

- Participate in the classroom newsgroup if necessary.

- Submit all assignments that are due, but be sure that you post them to the correct newsgroup folder.

- Read, if necessary.

Day 40 (Monday)

- Check the team newsgroup and work on team activities.

- Participate in the classroom newsgroup if necessary.

- Submit all assignments that are due, but be sure that you post them to the correct newsgroup folder.

- Read, if necessary.

Day 41 (Tuesday)

- Check the team newsgroup and work on team activities.

- Participate in the classroom newsgroup if necessary.

- Submit all assignments that are due, but be sure that you post them to the correct newsgroup folder.

- Read magazine articles and write your Learning Summary.

- Read, if necessary.

Day 42 (Wednesday)

- Check the team newsgroup and work on team activities.

- Submit all assignments that are due, but be sure that you post them to the correct newsgroup folder.

- Bid farewell to your classmates in the team and classroom newsgroups. Give thanks and kudos where appropriate.

Figure 2 is a schedule from an actual class. It is an excellent example of the general format for most classes. Obviously, each class is somewhat different because different subjects have different requirements.

The classes, for the most part, start fairly slow and give you a chance to acclimate to the subject, the teacher's instructional style, and the workload. This does not mean that complacency is feasible at anytime, because it is important for you to understand that it is very easy to fall behind, in a very short amount of time. Let me give you an example. For each day of participation, there may be approximately 30 to 50 messages from your classmates. It takes between an hour and an hour-and-a-half to read all of these and respond to approximately 4 of them. Don't forget that in order to stay enrolled in the class, the university rule is that you must post one message two out of seven days, but most instructors require that you post a *minimum* of two messages a day, five out of seven days each week. With an average of 40 messages a day, if you are five days behind, you can really hurt your grade for a class. It will also take you many hours to get caught up — approximately six hours just for postings; this does not include any other work that is due for the class.

Even if you are not the most knowledgeable person on the material, it is critical to maintain an active presence and visibility in the classroom newsgroup. This makes a better impression on the instructor. You don't need to be the brightest star, but you need to have a continual, noticeable presence (i.e., post messages every day!).

Figure 2: Typical schedule of assignments for a six-week course.

Day Due	Words	Pts	Actual	Post to Folder	Title of Assignment
Week One					
Thur/Fri Jan 8 & 9		0		Chat	Mini Autobiography
Fri–Wed 1/9–1/14	100	0		Classroom	Discussion Questions
Tues 1/13	350-700	5.0		Assignments (MSWord Attach)	1st Paper Due
Wed 1/14	100	5.0		Classroom	Weekly Learning Summary
Thurs–Wed 1/8-1/14	5 out of 7 days	5.0		Classroom	Participation
	Points	**15.0**			
Week Two					
Thurs–Wed 1/15–1/21	100	0		Classroom	Discussion Questions
Sun 1/18	Article Wk Sheet	5.0		Assignments	Individual Article Summary
Mon 1/19	250–500	5.0		Assignments (MSWord Attach)	Individual Paper Due
Tues 1/20	50	5.0		Learning Team & Assignments	Team Topic Selection
Wed 1/21	100	5.0		Classroom	Weekly Learning Summary
Thurs–Wed 1/15–1/21	5 out of 7 days	5.0		Classroom	Participation
	Points	**25.0**			

Figure 2: Typical schedule continued...

Day Due	Words	Pts	Actual	Post to Folder	Title of Assignment
Week Three					
Fri–Wed 1/22–1/28	100	0		Classroom	Discussion Questions
Mon 1/26	1,050–1,750	15.0		Assignments & Class Folder	Individual Paper Due
Tue 1/27	750–1,000	20.0		Assignments (MSWord Attach)	TeamArticle Report
Wed 1/28		10.0		Post E-Portfolio	Assessment and Bio
Wed 1/28	100	5.0		Main Classroom	Weekly Learning Summary
Thurs–Wed 1/22–1/28	5 out of 7 days	5.0		Main Classroom	Participation
	Points	**55.0**			
Week Four					
Fri–Wed 1/29–2/4		0		Chat	Discussion Questions
Sun 2/1	Article	5.0		Assignments	Individual Article Summary
Mon 2/2	100	0		Classroom	Team Assignment Due
Tue 2/3	350–700	10.0		Assignments (MSWord Attach)	Individual Paper Due
Wed 2/4	100	5.0		Classroom	Weekly Learning Summary
Thurs–Wed 1/29–2/4	5 out of 7 days	5.0		Classroom	Participation
	Points	**25.0**			

Figure 2: Typical schedule continued...

Day Due	Words	Pts	Actual	Post to Folder	Title of Assignment
Week Five					
Thurs–Wed 2/5–2/11	100	0		Classroom	Discussion Questions
Sun 2/8	Article	5.0		Assignments	Individual Article Summary
Mon 2/9	250–500	5.0		Assignments (MSWord Attach)	Individual Paper Due
Tues 2/10	50	5.0		Learning Team & Assignments	Team Assignment Due
Wed 12/11	100	5.0		Classroom	Weekly Learning Summary
Thurs–Wed 2/5–2/11	5 out of 7 days	5.0		Classroom	Participation
	Points	**25.0**			
Week Six					
Fri–Wed 2/13–2/18	100	0		Classroom	Discussion Questions
Mon 2/16	1,050–1,750	15.0		Assignments & Class Folder	Individual Paper Due
Tue 2/17	750–1,000	20.0		Assignments (Attach files)	Team Final Paper and PPT
Wed 2/18		10.0		Post E-Portfolio	Assignment
Wed 2/18	100	5.0		Main Classroom	Final Weekly Learning Summary
Thurs–Wed 2/12–2/18	5 out of 7 days	5.0		Main Classroom	Participation
	Points	**55.0**			
Course Total					

Chapter 6:

Instructors, Students, and Teams

What can I expect from the instructors?

Instructors in the online environment are easily as varied as the instructors in a brick-and-mortar institution, but there is one major difference. All of the instructors that I encountered in the online setting were actual professionals in their field. This was a truly refreshing aspect of online classes, but there are good and bad aspects to this.

A good aspect is that frequently these instructors can give you the real world take on different situations, and tell you how to handle these situations. They frequently have a vast amount of personal and academic resources that they can draw from. Most instructors have advanced degrees in the applicable field, or in a related field. The participation of instructors is usually fairly minimal, but instructors that spend more time on a class make students work harder than usual, but this is a good thing. This type of instructor can help you reach for the stars, and make it easier to see the interrelatedness of all things; he or she can be truly educationally inspirational.

The bad side of having professionals teach classes is that they may not be that well educated in the art of teaching, and may make some questionable calls when forced to deal with difficult situations. In the classes I was enrolled in, I found some mistakes in grading, but I confronted the instructors with the errors, and most of them rectified the mistakes. There were a few that did not, but I ended up with a good grade in the class anyway. There may be issues with the instructor's communication of expectations. Problems are usually a result of poor communication on the instructor's part, or an unclear explanation of expectations on assignments. If other students are unclear about the explanation of expectations then there is an obvious problem with the communication of the assignment. Some instructors may have too much going on personally and professionally, and may not be able to give timely feedback when it is needed to help define the direction for an upcoming assignment.

Instructors frequently refer to themselves as facilitator's, which leads me to believe that the university wants their role to be minimized. This is obvious with some instructors, but others are very involved. The instructors that are very interactive usually make the class much more interesting, but also make you work more by having you read and respond to more postings.

What can I expect from other students?

Students enrolled in Online College consist of U.S. residents or people with work visas working in the United States. They are working professionals that range in age from 30 to 60. This can be the best part of class; you can learn a great deal from all of these people. I met some wonderful people who were very knowledgeable in many different subject areas. Many were students that were part of the military and traveling abroad. This is rarely a problem in terms of class work. Most of these folks are very committed to their education, and make a diligent effort to contribute in a timely manner even if they are stationed overseas.

What are team interactions like?

Team interactions in an online environment are like no other team environment. My expectations of the online team environment were low and fraught with fears. Some of those fears did come true, but many were dispelled by the reality of the situation. Team interactions are a significant part of an online education and they enable you to get to know the good and bad sides of teammates. For the most part, interactions with team members are positive, but you may have some difficulties in the first few classes.

The problem with team interactions in an online environment is that they require you to have a great deal of trust in your teammates (whom you do not know and cannot see), and to keep the lines of communication open. If everyone does not interact regularly, or communicate on the same level, it can cause some trouble for the team as a whole. In my first class, confusion in the team setting occurred for two reasons: one person volunteered to do work that he did not do; and we set the deadline for individual team assignments too close to the project due date, which made a lot more work for the two participating team members. In my second class, there was a clash of ideas among team members regarding what was required on the assignment, how it should be carried out, who was going to do what, and so on. In my third class, the team was very small (three people) and one person did not pull her weight. After these first three classes, my team experiences really leveled out and became very routine, almost to the point of boredom on occasions. It takes at least three classes for many people to become accustomed to the routine of the online regimen, and the style of the program. The attrition rate among students is highest during the first three classes, but tends to even out after the fourth or fifth class.

This makes a lot of sense, especially after you have been in the program for a while and begin to get used to the way your life becomes acclimated to the classes. Another issue is that each student has a different working style. If you can accommodate the team, and get the planning aspects of the team assignments out of the way up front, then each person can tackle their part of the team assignments in the way that works best for them. Some people like to jump right in and get assignments completed, and others try to balance out their personal time, individual school work, and team workload, and work on projects as they arise. Then there are procrastinators that like to wait until the last minute for everything. None of these methods is necessarily wrong, but they each can have a dramatic impact on the team — especially if everyone on the team has a different working style. This is where it is imperative to have open communications so that everyone's expectations can be expressed.

In a couple of the classes I took, several members of the team were *very* driven and anxious to get team assignments done early in a very complete state. In almost every situation where this happened, the team ended up doing too much work, and occasionally even missed the real intention of the team assignment because there was too much emphasis on detail early on, and not enough attention paid to big-picture issues. These teams were very disappointing for me, because all of our hard work did not land us where we should have been. Fixing the problems was not feasible, because there simply was not enough time.

The best teams operate in the following manner:

- Have frequent and open communications between all team members and instructors

- Do a lot of planning up front

- Pay close attention to the requirements of each assignment

- Weigh issues carefully

- Give equal consideration to everyone's opinion

- Allow team members to deal with problems personally, before escalating matters

- Plan time for team interactions at critical junctures

- Rely on everyone equally

- Deal with most issues on consensus from the group

The personal growth that I experienced from team interactions was extremely high. In fact, team interaction came to be one of my favorite aspects of the program, but it was always something that required work — it was never easy.

Chapter 7:

Newsgroups: The Gateway to Communication

Newsgroups – what to write, what not to write

Above all, it is important to try and keep your interactions as friendly and professional as possible. Obviously, since all interactions are electronic, it can be difficult to know if someone is being intentionally rude, sarcastic, or obnoxious, and sometimes interactions can come off the wrong way.

It may be helpful to work out issues with a person over the phone, especially if you think that it is just a misunderstanding, and you believe that your message can be conveyed personally over the phone better than via e-mail or a newsgroup posting. Sometimes, contact of this nature is a necessity and can help the situation, but be careful not to escalate the situation.

It is also important to be as open-minded as possible when dealing with classmates. We all have good ideas, but sometimes compromise is more important than being right. This issue can become obscured by the fact that sometimes multiple students' grades are tied into the project. Patience and consensus building are frequently viewed as more important than a grade.

The primary classroom newsgroup

In the classroom newsgroup, it is important to keep your postings on topic, because that is the primary folder for classroom discussions. This is a challenge at times, because so many opportunities appear for discussions of relevant tangents. Most instructors allow them, but some may mention that you need to keep postings focused on the specific topic.

Many of the Discussion Questions cover personal experiences in the workplace regarding a particular topic. Not everyone has a lot of personal experiences to draw upon from a professional perspective and this may occasionally present difficulties, because the postings may be pretty limited. In situations like this, it is feasible to relate a similar experience while remaining on topic, and not get too focused on one particular experience.

This can be difficult to do at times, but will make the reading more enjoyable for your classmates.

Many instructors also have a hierarchical thread protocol (see Figure 3) that they want you to follow to post messages to facilitate the ability of all class members to follow common threads. For example, an instructor may want to see all responses to Discussion Question 1 under one common header. Most instructors that take the time to establish this protocol are militant about maintaining it, and not afraid to tell you when you digress. Accessing the class through the Web usually wreaks havoc with ones ability to maintain a hierarchical thread protocol.

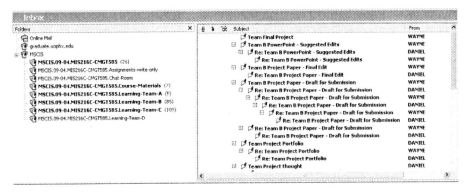

Figure 3: Hierarchical thread protocol.

Team Newsgroup

A team newsgroup is definitely different from a classroom newsgroup. All topics can be discussed here, but the instructor may comment if no work is being done, or if no discussions regarding work are occurring. This is also where you will experience the greatest potential for conflict in an online program. Be aware that sometimes the team newsgroup becomes a battleground when certain personalities interact. This is really where friendly and professional messages are the most important.

Another thing that is important is to frame your ideas for an assignment as a suggestion, and ask for feedback from the group. Demanding types of people that use commanding statements, frequently draw a great deal of resistance and rarely foster the cooperative environment that teams thrive on. That is not to say that friendly disagreements are not acceptable — they are — but war is unproductive. In your first online class, dealing with team dynamics is the primary topic addressed, and you will learn a lot about teams and team dynamics — theoretically and practically.

Chat room newsgroup

This is a forum for friendly; anything goes (G-rated) interaction. Sometimes this newsgroup gets a lot of interaction, but mainly only if there is a group that is particularly chatty and interactive.

Course materials and assignments newsgroups

These two groups are exactly what they say. Only instructors post course materials to the Course Materials newsgroup with students having read access. Only students post assignments to the Assignments newsgroup. The Assignments newsgroup is write only for students with no read access available. Instructors do have read access to the Assignments newsgroup.

Chapter 8:

Typical Online Document Types

Discussion Questions

Discussion Questions are usually questions that are on a pertinent topic, and specifically request that you address an issue within the topic with a personal experience or idea. An example of a Discussion Question is, "How does your organizational culture contribute to your job satisfaction? If it doesn't, how would you change the culture?" Discussion Question topics are generated from the reading assignments, or the instructor. They are enjoyable to respond to, and rarely difficult.

Papers

Papers, on the other hand, are usually challenging (no more than you would expect), but very interesting also. The accepted format for most papers is APA, but some instructors insist on MLA.

I've included an APA template on this book's accompanying Web site.

A trip to the local library to pick up some additional reference material may also help you to write papers a little more quickly. Most students in an online program use the Internet as a resource, which is allowed if properly cited as a reference, but not all of the material on the Internet is acceptable. Other sources are preferable.

The length of most papers is five to six pages, including the cover page and a reference page. This is not a great chore. The problem is to keep the length to three or four pages, because there is usually such an abundance of great material.

Weekly Summaries

Most instructors, but not all, require Weekly Summaries. A Weekly Summary is a 300 to 600-word document that describes what you learned that week. This is a challenging document at best, because it is next to impossible to write about everything that you learned with that many words. The best strategy is to just hit a topic in each area that struck you as interesting, controversial, or simply ridiculous.

Ideally, the Weekly Summary should include a paragraph or two on the following topics: the recommended reading of the textbook, additional texts read, the instructor's lecture, articles read, Discussion Questions, individual assignments, team assignments, and a brief epilogue.

Autobiographies

It is a great idea to just write a short (150 word) autobiography, because it will be used at the beginning of every class to help fellow students get to know you.

Chapter 9:

Who is a good candidate for online classes?

People that like to read, write, and are self-motivated are most likely to do the best in an online environment. The most important being self-motivation, then a love of writing. If you don't like to write, then this program could be a real drag, because writing is your primary means of communication.

What is the biggest challenge with online classes?

Team assignments and interactions are the most challenging part of online classes. While they do get easier with the passing of time, there are still plenty of unknowns from one class to the next. There are enough unknowns that could affect your life for six weeks, like it or not.

There is also an adjustment period of several classes until you can rather easily discern the general format for each class, and really get a handle on what is required. This means that the first week can be rather stressful in terms of feeling chaotic or disorganized due to a lack of understanding about what exactly is required for each class. Frequently, there are differences between the instructor's syllabus and the university document that outlines the class, which is called the *Unimodule*. In most cases, the syllabus takes precedence.

What is the easiest part of an online degree?

The easiest part of the classes is the reading. Not that it is always easy, but it is definitely always interesting. I also enjoyed writing papers for my classes because I learned so much from doing the research to write them.

How often do you have to log in to the class?

Most universities mandate that you log in to class at least twice a week to maintain your enrolled status. Most instructors require that you log in five days a week, and have at least two significant posts for each day. A significant post consists of an interactive response that is likely to be 50 to 100 words or more.

What format is used to conduct the class?

Most classes are conducted as a brick-and-mortar class would be. There are assigned reading and writing assignments. The teacher gives a weekly lecture and assigns Discussion Questions. The format will be familiar to most people.

What is the most frustrating part of online college?

Technology. I love technology and technology is what makes an online degree possible, but it can also be very frustrating. My advice is to hand all assignments in early, or at a time of day when the network traffic is light. Not everything always goes smoothly, and waiting until 11:59 P.M. to submit an assignment that is due at 12:00 A.M. is not wise. There are too many things that can go wrong. Get it done early, submit it, and move on.

Are Online Colleges as academically challenging as regular classes?

Online classes are as challenging as regular college classes, because they make you do as much work in 6 weeks instead of 16. In a regular classroom, you attend either two or three days per week, that is 32 or 48 meetings, and in an online class, if you log in and post messages five or seven days a week, that is 30 or 42 meetings. Most people post somewhere between 30 and 42 messages, especially in classes where the postings are heavy.

What is the best part of online college?

The best part of online college is that each class is six weeks, which is a very brief period of time and easy to tolerate. A 16-week semester is a sizeable amount of time and can feel like forever with certain classes, but 6 weeks is very manageable and over before you know it. Although, after 13 classes, I was getting burned out and was grateful to graduate.

Are Online Colleges accredited the same as regular universities?

This is an important point and I encourage you to investigate this matter for yourself and the school that you are interested in. Go to http://www.online-college.info/college-accreditation.htm and investigate the different types of accreditations that are recognized. This is an excellent Web site that offers a great deal of information. You can also visit the Higher Learning Commission at http://www.ncahigherlearningcommission.org/directory/index.php, or call or write to them at Higher Learning Commission, 30 N. LaSalle St., Suite 2400, Chicago, IL 60602-2504; 800-621-7440 or 312-263-0456; Fax: 312-263-7462.

Chapter 10:

Strategies for Online College Success

Personal scheduling and planning

After reading this book, you may think that Online College may be the direction for you to go. My advice is to always plan ahead. Plan ahead for each class. Try to get as much done as possible in advance of each class, and never wait until the last minute for anything. Procrastination in an online environment is dangerous, because of all of the things that can go wrong at the last minute that it is rarely worth waiting — especially when computers are involved.

Prepare your computer for emergencies

There is a product for computers, Norton Ghost, which makes an image of your computers' hard drive. I do not normally endorse products, but this product has saved me a tremendous amount of time and energy so many times that I cannot say enough about how great it is. It is more than worth the $50 to $70 that you will pay for it.

Norton Ghost can restore my system in 20 minutes and put a fresh copy of my hard drive back in place so that I can be up and running quickly. I use Norton Ghost to make an image of my primary C drive and make copies of my working files, which are on a drive partition on a CD-ROM.

Some classes you shine, some classes others shine

One last point about online classes is that it is easy to really excel in certain classes. As the class gets underway and you seem to click with the subject, assignments, instructor, and research, you may feel on top of your game and it will show. However, do not expect every class to be this way. Many may be, but most likely only a few classes will work out this well.

Epilogue

Getting any degree is a rewarding, but difficult endeavor. An online degree is no exception. I did not think that there would be an adjustment period upon completing an online degree, but there was. It has taken me several months to reclaim my "normal life". An extended vacation always facilitates a return to normalcy, quite nicely. I have only one caution: choose a degree program in an area of interest that you are passionate about, because it makes the long journey easier to take.

Good luck in your educational endeavors, whatever type they may be! Please visit http://www.virtualcollege.info for additional information regarding online college.

Disciaimer

This book was written from the vantage point of the author's experiences in an online college setting. The author makes no claims that you will have the same experience in any online class that you may take. Your experience in an online college may differ greatly, because each of our experiences are different and we percieve them differently. The author claims no responsibility for the experiences of others as it relates to their individual experiences in an online college class setting.

About the Author

Mark W. Timmis works as a writer and technical communications consultant for the IT industry in Indianapolis, Indiana. Mr. Timmis embarked on his "online" educational journey with the goal of obtaining a Masters of Science degree in Computer Information Systems, which he attained in October of 2003. Before coming to Indianapolis Mr. Timmis taught visual communications at the University of Evansville and Western Michigan University. Timmis wrote this book "Online College", and launched the accompanying website www.virtualcollege.info to help students navigate the "online system" in their quest for knowledge at virtual institutes of higher learning. If you have questions regarding the online college, drop Mr. Timmis a note at the email address on www.virtualcollege.info.